D

McConnell.

This book is due for return on or before the last date shown above: it may, subject to the book not being reserved by another reader, be renewed by personal application, post, or telephone, quoting this date and details of the book.

HAMPSHIRE COUNTY COUNCIL
County Library

Deckchairs III

Three one act plays

Jean McConnell

Samuel French — London
New York - Toronto - Hollywood

© 2001 BY JEAN MCCONNELL

Rights of Performance by Amateurs are controlled by Samuel French Ltd, 52 Fitzroy Street, London W1T 5JR, and they, or their authorized agents, issue licences to amateurs on payment of a fee. **It is an infringement of the Copyright to give any performance or public reading of the play before the fee has been paid and the licence issued.**

The Royalty Fee indicated below is subject to contract and subject to variation at the sole discretion of Samuel French Ltd.

Basic fee for each and every performance by amateurs in the British Isles — Code C (per play)

The Professional Rights in this play are controlled by SAMUEL FRENCH LTD.

The publication of this play does not imply that it is necessarily available for performance by amateurs or professionals, either in the British Isles or Overseas. Amateurs and professionals considering a production are strongly advised in their own interests to apply to the appropriate agents for written consent before starting rehearsals or booking a theatre or hall.

ISBN 0 573 10010 1

Please see page iv for further copyright information.

DECKCHAIRS III

Three one act plays:

Cupboard Love
Last Post
Cruise Missile

HAMPSHIRE COUNTY LIBRARY
P 1 X 200038303

COPYRIGHT INFORMATION

(See also page ii)

This play is fully protected under the Copyright Laws of the British Commonwealth of Nations, the United States of America and all countries of the Berne and Universal Copyright Conventions.

All rights including Stage, Motion Picture, Radio, Television, Public Reading, and Translation into Foreign Languages, are strictly reserved.

No part of this publication may lawfully be reproduced in ANY form or by any means—photocopying, typescript, recording (including video-recording), manuscript, electronic, mechanical, or otherwise—or be transmitted or stored in a retrieval system, without prior permission.

Licences for amateur performances are issued subject to the understanding that it shall be made clear in all advertising matter that the audience will witness an amateur performance; that the names of the authors of the plays shall be included on all programmes; and that the integrity of the authors' work will be preserved.

The Royalty Fee is subject to contract and subject to variation at the sole discretion of Samuel French Ltd.

In Theatres or Halls seating Four Hundred or more the fee will be subject to negotiation.

In Territories Overseas the fee quoted above may not apply. A fee will be quoted on application to our local authorized agent, or if there is no such agent, on application to Samuel French Ltd, London.

VIDEO-RECORDING OF AMATEUR PRODUCTIONS

Please note that the copyright laws governing video-recording are extremely complex and that it should not be assumed that any play may be video-recorded for whatever purpose without first obtaining the permission of the appropriate agents. The fact that a play is published by Samuel French Ltd does not indicate that video rights are available or that Samuel French Ltd controls such rights.

Other plays by Jean McConnell
published by Samuel French Ltd:

Deckchairs I
Deckchairs II
A Lovesome Thing

CUPBOARD LOVE

CHARACTERS

Peggy Higlett
Jane Frobisher

Scene — an esplanade at a seaside resort

Time — the present

The esplanade at a seaside resort. Early on a sunny morning

When the CURTAIN *rises, there are two beachchairs, facing* DS. *One is* LC, *the other* RC

Peggy jogs on from R. *She has clearly been jogging for some time but she chants "one-two, one-two" as she pegs gamely on. She wears jogging togs with a light bumbag, and a small towel around her neck. She crosses behind the chairs and jogs off* L

Jane appears from L. *She also has clearly been jogging for some time and chants "one-two, one-two". She wears jogging togs with a light bumbag, a head band, and a sweater tied around her waist. She jogs across the front of the chairs and off* R

Peggy jogs on UL *crosses to* R *and exits*

Jane jogs on UR *then exits* L

Peggy jogs on backwards from DR *to the nearest chair and leans on it to get her breath. She unties the towel round her neck and mops the sweat from her face*

Jane jogs on from UL. *She is clearly flagging too but she staggers on and exits* DL

Peggy is about to sit down but spots someone in the distance off stage. Jogging on the spot, she waves to the unseen person

Peggy (*calling off*) Hi, Samantha! Lovely morning!

Peggy ties her towel back round her neck and jogs off L, *just as Jane jogs on from* L *again*

Jane weaves her way to the R *but can go no further. She collapses in a chair* R

Peggy jogs on from L *to* R *very tired*

(*Calling off*) I'll carry on in a minute, Samantha! Stone in my shoe!

Jane I think she's gone.

Peggy dives for the chair L *and collapses into it. The two women gradually get their breath back*

Peggy I don't think she'd care if I had a stone in my kidney.
Jane Samantha? But she's a wonderful coach.
Peggy Agreed. But ruthless.
Jane Truly dedicated.
Peggy Having us out here — at dawn on a Sunday …
Jane Masses of qualifications — for PT.
Peggy Yes, yes, yes.
Jane Remarkable girl.
Peggy Are you related?
Jane No, no, no. I'm Jane Frobisher.
Peggy Peggy Higlett.

They stretch out to shake hands but can't quite reach. They wave limply at each other. Peggy takes off her trainer and empties it out. Jane finds a small bottle in her bag and takes a drink

I haven't seen you at the gym on Tuesdays.
Jane That's because I go on Thursdays.
Peggy Thursdays? Oh, I thought Thursdays was for the over ——
Jane Not necessarily! It's a more convenient day for me. I only joined recently.
Peggy Me too.
Jane Didn't know "Heavenly Bods " existed until a month ago. Found it in the *Yellow Pages*.
Peggy Me too. Needed to lose a spot of poundage!
Jane Me too. Thought my bathroom scales had gone mad. Just when I needed to look my best.
Peggy Me too. (*Coyly*) Got a wedding coming up.
Jane Granddaughter?
Peggy (*icily*) No. Mine.
Jane Sorry! I saw your ring …
Peggy I'm a widow.
Jane Sorry.
Peggy For a number of years now.
Jane So, when's the great day?
Peggy Not quite settled yet, actually.
Jane It's a bit of a coincidence because I'm thinking along similar lines.
Peggy Oh, lovely.
Jane Did you, by any chance, go to a marriage bureau?
Peggy A marriage bureau? Oh no, I couldn't do a thing like that.

Jane Me neither. It had passed through my mind. But no. These things need to come up naturally or not at all.
Peggy That's right.
Jane In my case it's been not at all.
Peggy Oh dear.
Jane Until now.
Peggy Well, he who dares wins!
Jane Quite! Go for it, eh?

The two women do a little more exercising, but without actually getting up from their seats

Peggy Just need a bit of toning up. It's difficult losing weight. I do love my food.
Jane I'm with you there.
Peggy One of life's pure pleasures my late husband used to say. As against the impure ones. Of which he was also a connoisseur. But it's not the same preparing meals for one.
Jane No, it's not.
Peggy Still I have had a very appreciative guest lately. I adore cooking! (*She bends low*)
Jane You've got a resurgence, you know.
Peggy (*with alarm*) Where?
Jane In interest. In cooking. All the programmes on TV. I love them.
Peggy Oh. Me too.
Jane Did you see the one on goose?
Peggy Goose? Now I have a very good way of using up goose fat. You know how fatty a goose can be …
Jane I'd prefer we didn't talk about fat.
Peggy You're not so fat.
Jane I didn't say I was. I'm big-boned.
Peggy Now there's a thing. You try getting a decent marrowbone nowadays. Never in the supermarkets. It's a wonder to me that the cattle can stand upright. I can see the future, herds of cows on crutches.
Jane And here, where have all the giblets gone?
Peggy You may well ask.

Jane looks off stage as if she has spotted Samantha in the distance

Jane Hi, Samantha! (*She rises*)
Peggy (*rising quickly*) Hi, Samantha!
Jane She works so hard.
Peggy She certainly does.

They both start bending and stretching energetically

Jane I've felt — so much better — since I began all this.
Peggy Me too.

Jane is toe-touching. Peggy stands on one leg, leaning against a chair with her eyes closed and hands pressed together. Jane sees her

Jane What sort of an exercise is that?
Peggy The Hindus do it.
Jane I doubt it. It's not one of Samantha's.

Peggy sniffs. But she also begins toe-touching. They ease off

Peggy Has she gone?
Jane (*taking a look between her legs*) Yes.

The two women clamber into their chairs again

Peggy I've a touch of cramp.
Jane My head band's a bit tight.
Peggy Very pretty colour.
Jane Thank you.
Peggy Mind you, I've made great strides since I began. I'll never forget my first session on the rowing machine. I was exhausted after thirty seconds!
Jane I think the rowing machine is meant for men, Piggy.
Peggy Peggy.
Jane Peggy. Sorry. Peggy.
Peggy Are you positive about the rowing machine?
Jane Think of the Eton Boating song. (*She sings*) "We'll all swing together, with our shoulders between our knees ..."
Peggy Are you sure those are the lyrics?
Jane Yes.
Peggy Sounds impossible.
Jane That's what I'm saying. It's not for women like us. Stick to the bicycle.
Peggy Oh, yes. I think that's rather jolly.
Jane And the walking machine.
Peggy And the vibrator.
Jane I don't think I've used that.
Peggy The belt that reduces your waist.
Jane Oh, that. I'm quite adept at the dumbbells.
Peggy The movement exercises are better. Especially if you have natural rhythm like me.

Jane They do go on a bit sometimes, though. But no gain without pain, Samantha says. I must say I enjoy the sauna.
Peggy Oh, yes!
Jane And the massage.
Peggy Gorgeous! I'm not sure which I prefer … Just lying there gently simmering …
Jane Or just lying there feeling kneaded.

They laugh

Peggy And then there's the snack bar.
Jane Oh, the snack bar! Mmm.
Peggy Definitely my favourite.
Jane They do a yummy baked potato with fillings various.
Peggy Oh, they do. The other day I had brie and walnuts with anchovy coulis.
Jane Have you tried the tuna with asparagus and sesame seeds?
Peggy I can really recommend the smoked ham with celery and boiled egg … Oh, watch out, there's Samantha! (*Calling off*) Yes, Samantha! Going on now! (*She waves off stage, to the unseen Samantha*)
Jane I think she's using binoculars.

The two women rise and jog separately round the stage. They speak breathily to each other as they pass

Peggy I did miss my Sunday fried breakfast ... Felt quite faint coming along the cliffs ... Found some blackberries.
Jane (*alert*) Blackberries?
Peggy Quite a lot — big — juicy …
Jane Where did you say they were?
Peggy Top of the steps — lot of bushes … Oh, God!

Peggy stops by the chairs. Jane continues jogging

Jane I'm sure we'll feel the benefit.
Peggy I'll feel the benefit when I sit down.
Jane You have to throw yourself into it or it's pointless.

Peggy contorts herself into another "Hindu" attitude

(*Jogging by*) I don't think that's much use.
Peggy Jane …
Jane Come on now.
Peggy Jane … Jane … Jane … I think I'm stuck.

Jane Serves you right.
Peggy Please — help!

Jane comes to Peggy's aid and unravels her limbs. Peggy collapses in her chair

Jane jogs off

(*Calling*) Come in number twelve your time's up!

Jane weaves back onstage, crosses to her chair and sinks down, giggling

Jane You are awful. I've lost my concentration.
Peggy I must have a break for a minute. Long enough for anybody. She has a sadistic streak, that Samantha.

Jane unties the sweater from her waist and puts it on. Peggy gets out a comb and mirror from her bumbag. They both tidy themselves up

You know I could have sworn I'd seen you before somewhere.
Jane You have. We've just been jogging along the esplanade together.
Peggy No, I mean somewhere quite different. I know! I've caught sight of you at the Adult Education Centre — the cordon bleu classes on Monday mornings, right?
Jane Your face is faintly familiar too.
Peggy I'm taking Mediterranean Meats with Mr Bertorelli.
Jane I'm taking Puddings and Pastry with Mrs Penticost. That's where it must have been.
Peggy Our paths must have crossed on the steps of the Adult Education Centre. I definitely have a vision of you carrying a casserole.
Jane I've always been interested in cookery. And now I have this added incentive.
Peggy Incentive?
Jane My gentleman friend.
Peggy Ah. So how did you meet your fiancé?
Jane I'd prefer you didn't call him that. It's not quite official. Just coming up to the boil.
Peggy I met *my* gentleman friend in the supermarket. He asked my advice about salmon en croute. He seemed so terribly lost.
Jane My friend lives round the corner. Some older men are helpless in the kitchen.
Peggy One feels so sorry. I think my friend spent many years overseas, with staff doing the cooking and chores. You know how it is.

Jane My friend said frozen meals were not a patch on his mother's home cooking. I ran round with some hot buttered scones, of course, straight from the oven. To cheer him up. He was so appreciative.

Peggy I met mine again in the supermarket, buying a tin of processed peas, would you believe. I explained about processed peas. And I invited him round for supper. I only did a simple roast with caramelized onions and parsnips and roast potatoes with sprouts and a little apple crumble with whipped cream. It was a delight to see him tucking in.

Jane I like to see a man enjoy his food. My gentleman friend loves steak and kidney pudding.

Peggy I've yet to find a man who doesn't like his puddings. Jam roly-poly or spotted dick with nice rich custard. It's no wonder I've put on the pounds. So has he!

Jane Nice to have a dinner guest.

Peggy Nice to entertain again.

Jane My friend loves to be taken by surprise.

Peggy What do you do — jump out on him?

Jane Jump out on him? No, no. I don't do anything like that.

Peggy Sorry.

Jane I mean he likes me to take chances — to experiment.

Peggy Oh ho.

Jane In the kitchen.

Peggy Of course. So what are you cooking for him today?

Jane Smoked haddock in cheddar cheese sauce on a bed of frothy scrambled eggs with herby potato croquettes. To start. Then crown of beef with assorted veg and rum baba to follow.

Peggy Delicious. I'm putting some venison cutlets in an overnight marinade of Madeira, marmalade and red scallions.

Jane That sounds very rich.

Peggy Oh, it is. My own recipe of course. Served with fondant baby turnips and crispy bacon stuffed aubergines.

Jane I made quite a hit with my Profiteroles St Honoré. Mrs Penticost was so helpful to me with the spun sugar halo. My friend said it looked quite bridal. That was a naughty hint, don't you think?

Peggy Definitely. Mr Bertorelli has been an inspiration. I was so impressed when he showed us his Cortina medallions.

Jane He was in the Italian army?

Peggy No no, medallions of Lucca lamb in Chianti and sundried tomato, pesto and coriander polenta.

Jane Ah.

Peggy Mr Bertorelli is full of ideas. But he encourages us to use our own initiative. He was knocked out by my pig's trotters in a blanket. Particularly since I used old fashioned grey pepper. He said he was so bored with those freshly ground black peppercorns.

Jane I must go to his class next term. He sounds inspiring.
Peggy You obviously have a flair.
Jane Thank you. I can see you are something of a culinary artist yourself.
Peggy Thank you. I'm so glad we met, having so much in common.
Jane Right. We must keep in touch — exchange tips.
Peggy We must.
Jane My friend says he doesn't know how I manage to be so inventive. But it's worth every bit of effort — just to see him trying to identify some unusual ingredient … We have quite a little guessing game sometimes.
Peggy Occasionally my friend muddles my cooking with his mother's and I take that as a compliment. Told me he had never tasted a hare terrine to beat mine.
Jane Well I never.
Peggy The odd thing was I had never cooked him a hare terrine. Never cooked a hare terrine in my life! Wished I had.
Jane Don't worry. I'll give you my recipe. Hare terrine is my speciality.
Peggy Thank you.
Jane Funny. I had a similar thing happen. My friend said he loved my galantine of tongue. When I pointed out it was pork brawn, he said it must have been a slip of the tongue. How we laughed.
Peggy Galantine of tongue is one of my particular things. It is so good to meet a kindred spirit.

They pull their chairs nearer to each other

I'm sure you are just the person to ask. Tell me have you been able to find any decent plaice?
Jane Decent place for what? The reception?
Peggy What? No, no. Plaice, plaice!
Jane I can hear you! Oh, you mean the fish? I get you.
Peggy Nothing like it once upon a time. Nowadays they're caught before they're old enough to leave their mother.
Jane I agree. And if you raise the question they just wave a seabass at you.
Peggy I blame the government.
Jane Which one?
Peggy All of them!
Jane I'll give you my recipe for Tibetan kipper dumplings. That'll cheer you up.
Peggy And I'll return the compliment with my banoffee tiger prawn.
Jane How kind.
Peggy I can see our minds run along similar tracks.
Jane It's the sense of triumph when you know you've concocted a truly startling yet finely-balanced menu ——

Peggy A gastronomic achievement …
Jane ——and you bask in the warm glow of approbation.
Peggy When he gazes at you over his empty plate, sighing with contentment, mopping those tiny flecks from round his mouth, easing a notch of his belt, with nothing but murmurs of wonder and admiration.
Jane Wonder and admiration.

The two women sigh happily. A pause

Peggy Has your gentleman friend moved in with you?
Jane Oh, no. Not yet. But he comes round to me regularly three evenings a week.
Peggy Three evenings a week?
Jane Oh yes, for some months now. As I said, getting quite serious. There was one break for a while when he had flu. And had to stay away. He wouldn't dream of letting me come near him. I tried to deliver something nourishing to his door. But he wouldn't let me over the threshold. So considerate.
Peggy Very. No-one needs flu.
Jane Still it wasn't too long and we were back to our usual evenings together. Tuesdays, Thursdays and Saturdays. And alternate Sundays for lunch.

A little pause

Do you see your gentleman friend frequently?

There is another pause

Peggy Three evenings a week.
Jane Oh.

Another pause

Peggy Mondays, Wednesdays and Fridays.

Another pause

Jane (*weakly*) Mondays, Wednesdays and Fridays?
Peggy That's what I said. And alternate Sundays for lunch.

There is a very long pause

Jane Alternate Sundays for lunch.

The two women stiffen as the truth dawns. They move their chairs apart again. Battle is drawn

Peggy (*at last*) Well! I think we know where we stand.
Jane (*coldly*) I think we do.
Peggy Clearly he needed to get the taste of your cooking out of his mouth!
Jane Really! Don't you expect to get my hare terrine recipe!
Peggy I wouldn't dream of touching it. Excuse me!

Peggy rises moves aside and continues her exercises. Jane rises and moves to the other side and does the same. They work-out in silence for a moment or two. Then continue conversing without looking at each other

Jane Obviously he only befriended you out of the kindness of his heart — knowing you to be a widow — otherwise he would have eaten with me *every* evening.
Peggy Huh! That would have been the finish of him. All your sickly puddings! No wonder he was thankful for my salads …
Jane With pickled walnut and blue cheese and fried crouton dressing and a dollop of mayonnaise.
Peggy How revolting!
Jane I wouldn't put it past you! Preying on the poor lonely man's needs!
Peggy You were in there fast enough with your hot scones.
Jane He said I knew how to tickle his taste buds.
Peggy He said I knew how to awaken his appetite. Exhausted after all your tickling!
Jane He said Tuesdays, Thursdays and Saturdays were the highspots of his week.
Peggy He said Mondays, Wednesdays and Fridays were his favourite evenings.
Jane I said he was welcome to come to Sunday lunch any time. But he said he had to make a special visit every fortnight.
Peggy You see! *My* Sunday lunches were special!
Jane The visits were to his mother's grave.
Peggy No, he visited that every other Sunday.

There is another pause. They stop exercising. Peggy takes her lipstick out and makes up defiantly. Jane folds her arms scornfully

Jane I thought you said your gentleman friend had named the day.
Peggy I said no such thing.
Jane In so many words.
Peggy We have an understanding.

Jane Really? Maybe the understanding is all on your side.
Peggy We have become very close indeed.
Jane And so have we, so there! In fact only last night he looked into my eyes very meaningfully. No mistaking what was in his mind.
Peggy Huh! We've gone a lot further than meaningful looks!
Jane How much further?
Peggy He presses my hands very ardently when we part. And we've kissed!
Jane Huh! *We've* kissed.
Peggy We've kissed ardently!
Jane Ardently? Another slip of the tongue, I suppose!
Peggy Really! (*She turns away*) Excuse me!
Jane And excuse me! I am on a personal training schedule with Samantha. Her pre-nuptial programme!

Jane jogs off R

Peggy (*calling after her*) She'll have her work cut out!

Peggy jogs to L *then back to* C

Jane jogs on from R *to* C

They come to a halt and face each other squarely

I think I've just remembered where we met before.
Jane Where who met before?
Peggy You and I.
Jane On the steps of the Adult Education Centre …
Peggy No, on the doorstep of *his* house. When he had that flu.
Jane Flu?
Peggy We came face to face. Just as he opened the door in his dressing-gown.
Jane You know, I do believe I recall it too. Yes. I do. You were delivering Meals on Wheels.
Peggy I was *not* delivering Meals on Wheels. It was French onion soup. It was *you* delivering Meals on Wheels.
Jane I certainly was not. It was a leg of beef casserole.
Peggy There! I knew it was a casserole.

They glare at each other

Jane He told me you were Meals on Wheels.
Peggy He told me *you* were Meals on Wheels.
Jane But he told me *quite definitely* ——

Peggy *Quite definitely* — that *you* were Meals on Wheels.

The two women turn and sit down in their seats. Silently they stare out front as the enormity of the deception dawns on them. A long pause

I understand now about the hare terrine.
Jane (*nodding*) And I understand about the galantine of tongue. A slip of the tongue. Huh!

The two women sigh dejectedly

Peggy You have to hand it to him, he certainly kept a very careful engagement diary.
Jane He must have thought he was in paradise.
Peggy Bliss on a stick.
Jane No wonder he's put on all that weight. Twice as much as I have.
Peggy And twice as much as I have. I suppose that figures.
Jane There he was saying he needed a new suit. I thought it was for the wedding. I see now he was bursting at the seams. What a trick, leading me on like that! Ooh! I could kill him!
Peggy (*thoughtfully*) I think we're already doing a good job there.
Jane Well, he's eaten his last Beef Wellington in my house. If he comes near again he'll get the boot Wellington.
Peggy (*thoughtfully*) No. I think we should carry on just as we are.
Jane What! He's not getting away with it!
Peggy Trust me. We should go on feeding him with all the richest, fattest, sweetest dishes we can find. We'll invent ever more exotic extravagances, drenched in liqueurs …
Jane I'm getting your drift.
Peggy I'll top him up one night ——
Jane — and I'll top him up the next.
Peggy The way to a man's heart-attack is through his stomach!
Jane Is that kind?
Peggy He's free to refuse.
Jane But he won't.
Peggy He'll go on chomping away on the more and more spicy delights from my oven and your oven. Into his willing jaws ——
Jane — and down into his swelling stomach ——
Peggy — and on to his expanding body by way of his thickening arteries ——
Jane — and his long-suffering liver ——
Peggy — and his withering kidneys ——
Jane — and his pulverized pancreas ——
Peggy — and when he's taken to hospital and put on a diet, we'll smuggle in the tiny titbits. Home-made coconut ice ——

Jane Little sponge fingers soaked in brandy; he loves those. Are we being mean?

Peggy He's free to refuse.

Jane But he won't.

Peggy He'll never guess he's been rumbled until we stand side by side together before him on his deathbed.

Jane Oh, you are naughty!

Peggy It might be enough to confront him arm-in-arm and tell him the jig is up.

Jane More than enough probably. Oh dear, it does seem a shame. I did so enjoy the cordon bleu classes and all that …

Peggy Yes, that's the down side. Mr Bertorelli was doing spit-roast leg of kid next week.

Jane Really?

Peggy Yes. I think we should go on with the classes.

Jane Yes. (*Pausing thoughtfully*) But it wasn't just the cooking. It was the praise. The compliments. The plaudits! Just seeing him wriggling in anticipation as I lifted the lid.

Peggy (*nodding*) Drooling …

Jane Knife and fork at the ready …

Peggy I do know what you mean.

Jane Listen, Piggy—Peggy. I have an idea. Suppose you came round to me on Tuesdays, Thursdays and Saturdays …

Peggy And you came to me on Mondays, Wednesdays and Fridays … ! (*She stops*) No, it wouldn't work. We need a wider audience.

Jane (*nodding*) The roar of the crowd. The smell of the grease … I mean the fragrance wafting from the kitchen …

Peggy The kitchen of our tiny very exclusive high-class restaurant.

Jane You mean … Are you suggesting …?

Peggy Our very own establishment.

Jane Together?

Peggy Why not? With our very own specialities and our very own clientele clamouring for one of our six tables.

Jane Six?

Peggy Maybe just four. I cook Monday, Wednesday and Friday and you cook Tuesday, Thursday and Saturday.

Jane (*with delight*) Heaven! Oh, Peggy! What will we call it?

Peggy We'll call it Cupboard Love!

The two women roar with laughter. Jane spots Samantha again

Jane Oh, look who's back. (*She waves off*) Hi, Samantha!

Peggy (*waving off*) Hi, Samantha! (*She rises*)

Jane (*surprised*) We're not jogging any more are we?

Peggy Of course we are. Round to the pub to celebrate!
Jane (*rising*) That's more like it!

They tog up, link arms and then jog side by side once round the stage, waving as they go

Bye, Samantha! One-two … One-two …
Peggy Bye, Samantha! One-two ... One-two …

They exit

The CURTAIN *falls*

LAST POST

CHARACTERS

Felicity Grant-Poole
Mary O'Riley

Scene — the garden of the Grant-Pooles' seaside holiday house
Time — the present

The garden of the Grant-Pooles' seaside holiday house. It is a bright summer's day

When the CURTAIN *rises, there is a garden table,* C*, with a beach chair either side of it. On the table is set a tray with a small coffee percolator, a pretty cup and saucer, milk jug and sugar. Unseen as yet, far* DSR*, there is a chair and a small table*

Felicity Grant-Poole enters L*. She is in her sixties, dressed in an elegant summer dress and sunhat. She wears a locket round her neck. She carries several unopened letters, one of which is a blue envelope; a copy of* The Times *newspaper and a cordless telephone. She places them all on the table and sits down on the chair* R *of it. Her manner is subdued*

Felicity takes up the percolator and automatically goes to pour as if there is a cup on the opposite side of the table. She stops herself with a little sigh, collects herself together, then pours her own cup of coffee and adds the milk and sugar. She begins to open her mail, occasionally taking a drink of coffee. The first letter is obviously junk mail. Felicity just pushes it aside. The second letter she opens and begins to read

The telephone rings. Felicity picks up her cordless telephone

Felicity (*into the telephone*) Hallo? ... (*Relaxing*) Oh, hallo, darling. How are you? ... Yes, I'm fine. Truly. You don't need to call me every day now, dear. I know you're busy. We've all got to get on with our lives, my love. That's what Daddy would have wanted. ... We've all got to be brave soldiers, right? ... I'm managing very well, honestly. Mrs Beggs comes in most days and makes herself useful. She's a good soul. Always cheerful. She misses Dad too, you know. She said the other day, quite out of the blue, "We were lucky to have the Colonel as long as we did, madam." That was sweet, don't you think? She has a very warm heart. I've had so many letters. Such kind words. I think there are more here in the mail today. Some from overseas. From fellow officers, I expect — who served with him. Only just heard, I suppose. ... I know it was all in *The Times*, dear. But there are still places in the world where *The Times* doesn't penetrate. ... (*Chuckling*) Outer Mongolia, darling. I have a few here addressed to Daddy. ... No, darling, I'd better just glance through them. I should just drop the people a line. It's all right, sweetheart. I'm not a complete wimp. ...(*She laughs*)

Quite! Give the babes a big hug from me. I'll see you all the weekend after next. ... What? ... I am perfectly OK! Louise meets me most days to walk the dogs. The weather's lovely. You'll be able to swim, I think. Yes. ... Bye now! ... You too, my love. (*She puts the phone aside, takes another drink of coffee and picks up the letter again. She reads it with a gentle smile*)

The telephone rings. Felicity answers it

(*Into the telephone*) Hallo? Oh, Louise, hallo. ... Fine! Are we meeting later? On the beach as usual? ... Good. Just opening the mail. There is such a wonderful letter from the Regiment. You know they commissioned a portrait of Edward last year. They want to have a little ceremony — a sort of dedication to his memory. It was such a good picture. It's to hang in the Mess. They say, (*reading from the letter*) "The colonel was admired and respected by his fellow officers and the men alike, both as a soldier and as a man of true honour." Isn't that splendid, Louise? I think they mean it. Well, see you later on. ... Yes. ... When the tide's full out. Bye! (*She puts the letter aside and takes another drink of coffee. She spots the letter with the blue envelope on the pile and is intrigued. She removes it from the others, turns it over and studies the address on the back. She is puzzled*)

Mary O'Riley enters far DR. *She is in her forties and is dressed casually. She carries a pen, a blue notepad and envelope*

As Mary enters, a spotlight comes up on her and lights the small table and chair DR

Mary sits at the little table and begins writing a letter. Felicity opens the envelope, takes out the letter and silently reads

Mary (*with a soft Irish accent; writing*) Dear Eddie, I'm so worried. What has happened? The usual date had come and gone with no communication from you whatever. This is the very first time you have ever let me down. Oh dear, you see how much I have come to rely on your dear kind nature. (*She pauses*)

Felicity stops reading. She finds the envelope, looks at it again and goes on silently reading the letter

(*Writing*) I would never have written to you. You know I have kept my word. But the matter is urgent. It is about little Teddie. In the last month I have been told there is a surgeon in America, who has perfected a special operation. An operation which could mean that Teddie might be able to walk. I know you will understand what this means to the boy. And I am sure it would make you happy to think he could at last run and play and have fun like other children. (*She carries on writing in silence*)

Felicity (*reading the letter aloud*) "You know I have always paid up on the insurance you took out for us. As you appreciated, Teddie's condition involved me in so much expense. But this new operation, while it sounds like some kind of miracle, will cost far more than the policy will cover. Teddie is thrilled, and not at all scared. But you know he is a brave kid. How could he not be, with such a father ..." (*She breaks off with a gasp and then carries on reading in silence*)

Mary (*writing*) There must have been some mistake — the bank or the post, I don't know — as I am sure you would never want us to be in this situation. You know how grateful I have always been for your attitude to things. And you know I wouldn't be writing to you now if it wasn't so urgent and so important right at this moment to little Teddie. (*She signs the letter*)

Felicity (*reading aloud*) "As always, Mary O'Riley." (*Stunned*) As — always — Mary O'Riley.

Mary puts the letter in a blue envelope, seals it and exits R

The spotlight fades out, DR

The letter Felicity has been reading falls from her hand

Oh, my God. (*With distress*) My — God. It can't be possible ... (*She picks up the letter and reads it through again silently. She puts the letter aside. She is very upset. Slowly, she opens the locket she is wearing, stares at it and begins to cry. She picks up the telephone and taps a number. She finds a handkerchief and mops her face. Into the phone*) Louise? Louise — something terrible's happened. I have a letter here. Addressed to Edward. It's from a woman. She obviously doesn't know he's dead. She's got a child, Louise. She's got Edward's child. She's got a little boy. Edward's son. ...(*She weeps again, but is listening to the person speaking to her*) Oh, Louise, it's obvious. He's been supporting them. Why else? ... I know. I find it impossible to believe. They must have been lovers. ... Oh, Louise, don't! She *must* have been! ... I don't *know* when! Or where! I've never had the slightest suspicion! I've always trusted him implicitly. (*She cries again, then she pulls herself together*) Louise, listen to me. No-one is to know about this. Do you understand? Particularly not the girls. Nor anyone of his Regiment. They all believed in him. I don't want that to be changed, whatever happens. I wouldn't even have told you, Louise, but it was such a shock. Will you give me your solemn word? ... Thank you. I know I can trust you. Louise, I don't want to talk any more right now. You understand? Bye. (*She puts the phone down. She sits a moment, staring into space, holding the locket to her cheek*)

Felicity collects the other letters on to the tray, leaving Mary's letter and envelope on the table. She carries the tray and exits L

The spotlight comes on, DR

Far DR, *Mary enters, wearing a jacket. She is carrying a cream-coloured unopened letter, blue notepaper and pen which she puts on the table. She takes off her jacket and hangs it on the chair. She sits and looks at the envelope*

Felicity enters L *with a pen, cream notepaper and envelope. She sits at the table and begins to write*

Mary opens the letter, as Felicity writes

Felicity (*writing*) Dear Miss O'Riley, your letter to Colonel Grant-Poole has come into my hands.

Mary (*reading*) "This has occurred because the colonel, my husband, died three months ago, and, as his widow, correspondence has been delivered to me. You obviously have not been informed of his death."

Felicity (*writing*) I am sorry for the necessity of writing to you with this unexpected news. (*She pauses*) May I say, I hope you will keep this matter completely confidential. As I myself intend to do.

Mary (*reading*) "I hope you will keep this matter completely confidential. As I myself intend to do."

Felicity } **Mary** } (*together as Felicity signs the letter*) Felicity Grant-Poole.

Felicity writes the envelope, referring to Mary's letter for the address. Mary sits staring at the letter, then faces out front, pondering. Felicity seals the envelope

Felicity rises carrying the letters and exits L

Mary sets the letter aside and takes up her blue notepad and begins to write. She writes half a dozen lines, then she halts, pauses in thought and looks again at the letter from Felicity. Then she picks up the letter she had begun and crumples it up. She rises and puts on her jacket

Mary exits DR

The spotlight fades out, DR

Mary enters R *into the main area. She carries a handbag and a copy of the* Telegraph. *She puts them both on the table* C *and perches on the chair* R *of it. She looks about the place, and appears ill-at-ease. Mary rises*

Felicity enters from L. *She is wearing a different dress. She is carrying her coffee tray with letters, phone and* The Times *newspaper as usual*

Felicity (*calling back to her housekeeper off* L, *controlling her voice to its normal tone*) Yes, Mrs Beggs, everything is all right. No, don't worry about another coffee cup. I'd sooner you went down to the village right away. We're fine here in the garden. No need to hurry back, Mrs Beggs. (*She crosses to the table and puts down the tray*)
Mary I'm sorry if this is an inconvenient time to call.

Felicity just stands staring at Mary

A door slams, off. Felicity glances back off stage to register that her housekeeper has gone out. She advances on Mary, in a blazing fury

Felicity How dare you come here! How dare you!
Mary But you showed me in, so I thought ——
Felicity My housekeeper was standing there in the hall. What else could I do! I was certainly not going to allow a scene in front of her!
Mary I don't intend to make a scene …
Felicity You certainly won't! I would be grateful if you would kindly leave my house at once!
Mary I'm sorry …
Felicity How you have the gall to turn up on my doorstep!
Mary You don't understand! When I got your letter I ——
Felicity I wrote to you out of simple courtesy. It was not an invitation to visit! Surely you might have repaid my note to you by showing similar good manners — and making no further contact.
Mary I did appreciate that letter.
Felicity It was difficult enough to write in all conscience!
Mary I understand. It must have been.
Felicity You don't understand a bit. You have no idea!
Mary Mrs Poole — er, Grant-Poole— the last thing I wanted to do was distress you.
Felicity That's rich!
Mary I think I've made a mistake coming. Perhaps I shouldn't have come at all. But I so wanted to put some things right.
Felicity I doubt whether that's possible.

Mary Please let me stay a few minutes. I needed to get up all my courage to knock on your door. I walked up and down the road. I walked up and down the beach. I started back for the station — then I realized that what I had to do was terribly important. But I'll go right now if you insist.

Felicity is silent. Her passion has exhausted her. She sits in the chair L *of the table. She closes her eyes for a moment and breathes deeply. Mary moves to the table*

Mary (*anxiously*) Are you ill?
Felicity (*immediately*) No!
Mary (*gently*) I know what you must be feeling.
Felicity I can't imagine that you do.
Mary It was good of you to let me in.
Felicity I hardly had a choice.
Mary You could have slammed the door in my face.
Felicity I was certainly tempted.

There is another pause. Felicity regards Mary keenly, taking the woman in properly for the first time. Mary stands waiting awkwardly. At last Felicity points to the chair R *of the table. Mary sits*

Mary Believe me, my first thought when I got your letter telling me about Ed … (*Correcting herself*) About the colonel. Well — after my initial shock I straightaway thought what a shock it must have been for you to read my letter.
Felicity I found it very hard to believe. I still do.
Mary That's the point. I want so very much to ease things for you.
Felicity You can't think calling here could do that!
Mary Please do hear me out. I really need to explain the circumstances — the situation.
Felicity I think those are fairly obvious.
Mary It was such a very brief relationship. Hardly a relationship at all.
Felicity Is this meant to make me feel better?
Mary What I'm saying is it was not important.
Felicity Not to you perhaps. But I knew my husband. He would never have taken any relationship lightly.
Mary I suppose I'd like to think I meant a little to him. But it truly was so fleeting …
Felicity But what about your child?
Mary If that terrible mistake hadn't happened then Ed — the colonel — would never have made contact again. It was over. There were never any deep feelings.

Felicity When did this happen? Where did it happen?

Mary I won't tell you any details. That will make it far more important than it was.

Felicity I'd still like to know.

Mary So that you can brood on it? No, I'll never tell you anything more.

Felicity You're right. I don't want to know. I want the whole thing to disappear!

Mary It would never have mattered ——

Felicity To me it would!

Mary You would never have known. Your husband would have put it to the back of his mind. Forgotten it completely. No man is entirely perfect.

Felicity So it seems.

Mary Don't be bitter. That's why I came here, don't you see? To try to stop you getting it all out of proportion. Letting it spoil your memories of your husband. You had a good marriage?

Felicity So I believed.

Mary I feel guilty enough as it is bringing this on you. You mustn't let it be ruined by my thoughtless letter. Oh, why did I write it? I'd given my word!

Felicity He pledged you to secrecy. To deceit.

Mary It was for the best ...

Felicity It was dishonest. I can't recognize Edward in all this. I can't see it in his character.

Mary No-one is perfect. No-one in this world. You must know that. Such a person doesn't exist.

Felicity I thought I knew Edward through and through.

Mary Can't you allow him the littlest flaw?

Felicity Little! How long did the *affaire* go on?

Mary It was not an *affaire*. It was an unguarded moment. Ships passing in the night ...

Felicity Oh please!

Mary The whole thing would have been unimportant — if little Teddie hadn't been born.

Felicity How do you know he was Edward's?

Mary (*quietly*) There was no question.

Felicity I'm sorry. That was insulting.

Mary Yes it was. But I understand what you are going through. I would like you to understand what I was going through — the panic I was in. It's a fact I could have coped with the baby, with help from my family and from some good friends. But when it transpired that ... When it came to light that ... That little Teddie was — was ... (*She breaks off, tears coming*) I'm sorry.

There is silence between the two women as Mary fumbles for a handkerchief in her bag, then pocket, then sleeve. She hasn't one. Felicity takes a handkerchief from her own pocket and offers it. Mary takes it and presses it to her face. At last she recovers and offers the handkerchief back. Felicity ignores it

Mary Do you have children?

Felicity Don't you know? No. I suppose that isn't the sort of thing you talked about in bed. Or wherever you were …

Mary (*after a pause*) There doesn't seem to be anything I can say to make sense of it to you.

Felicity I don't think there is. And I certainly don't want to discuss my daughters. They will never know anything about this. Ever!

Mary Of course not. All I meant to say was that if you were a mother — a mother of strong and healthy children …

Felicity Thank God, they are. So are my grandchildren. And I hope they will never know a word about this matter. They adored their grandfather.

Mary I swear to you I would never have contacted the colonel again. But when it was obvious my boy was going to need my nursing care full-time — and there were going to be a great many expenses … Well, one day when I was at my lowest, I wrote him a note. I wasn't even sure it would reach him. But somehow it did.

There is another pause

Felicity What were you hoping for?

Mary I don't know … Not to see him, I swear! Not to complicate his life. I just needed a bit of help. And I knew … I suppose I just knew he wouldn't refuse to give it.

Felicity That Edward would never refuse to do the decent thing? Yes, that sounds like him. If nothing else does.

Mary So he … Well …

Felicity It's clear he made you an allowance.

Mary For the boy. It made all the difference in the world to our lives. I was very careful. I'd even saved a bit of it. Everything I spent was in order to make little Teddie's life a better one. As far as it was possible. Then this quarter it didn't arrive …

Felicity (*quietly*) No, of course not.

Mary And it was ironic because it was when I had suddenly found out about this surgeon in America. A friend cut an article out of a newspaper and sent it to me. I couldn't believe it was true at first — that there was a way that little Teddie might be able to live a normal life. Go to school. I'd be able to go to work again. The thought of it … Then Ed's cheque didn't arrive and I couldn't understand. I wrote at last in desperation, you must see. I knew if he realized the money had gone astray he would deal with it at once.

Now of course I know why … But I shouldn't have written the letter. I had given my word. I just hope you can understand and forgive me.

Felicity I suppose I understand. I've never been in your situation.

Mary That's kind of you. I know the colonel's support was more than I deserved. But he did it for the sake of little Teddie who is just an innocent victim. He is such a good little boy.

Felicity Where does he think his father is?

Mary He's always believed his father is dead … (*She breaks off*)

A pause

Felicity Yes. Well …

Mary I'm sorry, but I had to come. To put things right — as right as I could. Believe me, I will never contact you again. Or ever mention it to anyone at all. The last thing I would want is for Ed's reputation to suffer in any way. He was a good, kind, thoughtful man. Of great integrity.

Felicity He was.

Mary (*rising*) I'm going now.

Felicity I think you'd better. In case my housekeeper comes back. I could never allow her to get a hint of this. She worshipped the colonel. Everyone who ever knew him did. And I have no intention of letting anyone ever think less of him.

Mary I'll never say a word, I swear to God. Do you believe me?

Felicity I hope I can.

Mary And I hope you have forgiven me for coming to see you. I meant it for the best.

Felicity You came a long way.

Mary I had to come over to England to see a specialist about this operation for little Teddie. We stayed with a friend in London. We'll be going back home tomorrow.

Felicity So what will happen to the child?

Mary We'll go on as we are. We'll manage. It was always Ed who insisted. It was always for the boy. Everything Ed did was for Teddie.

Felicity I can imagine that. He was very fond of children. He idolized the girls. (*Thoughtfully*) How could he have felt when he thought of a child being crippled for life …?

Mary (*after a pause*) I must go now.

Felicity Wait. Wait here.

Felicity exits quickly L

Mary Right. I understand. I'll stay until you see the coast is clear.

Felicity returns instantly, carrying her handbag. She hurries to the table, sits, opens the bag and takes out a cheque book and pen

Felicity (*writing*) I think I know what my husband would have liked me to do.
Mary But please …
Felicity No. I'm as sure as if he were here to tell me. I know it as clearly as if he were looking at me with his honest eyes and speaking to me in his deep, calm voice. (*She writes the cheque*) Mary O'Riley. Right? Here!

Felicity holds out the cheque. Mary sees the figure and gasps

Felicity I know the sort of cost involved for medical treatment in the States.
Mary But such a sum! You really mustn't!
Felicity I am lucky enough to have money. Take it.
Mary (*taking the cheque*) How can I ever thank you! How can little Teddie ever thank you …
Felicity Don't say any more. I thought I heard someone! Please go out through the garden gate!

Flustered, Mary takes up her bag and stuffs the cheque in it. She grabs up The Times *and starts off* R

Mary Goodbye!
Felicity We shall not meet again.
Mary No. Goodbye. And thank you!

Mary exits R

Felicity sinks back in her chair. She is spent. Then she realizes Mary has inadvertently taken The Times *instead of her* Telegraph

Felicity (*rising to* R) Miss O'Riley, you've left your newspaper … You've taken mine …

But Mary is gone. Felicity glances off L. *She realizes she must appear normal for her housekeeper's benefit. She pours herself a coffee and reaches for Mary's* Telegraph. *She finds that the newspaper is folded back at the Obituaries page. She begins to read*

The spotlight comes up, DR

Mary enters DR *carrying a holdall. She is not wearing her jacket now. From*

the holdall she takes out the Telegraph*, a marker pen and a notepad and pencil. She sits at the small table and studies the obituaries page. She is very business-like*

Mary (*reading*) "Robert Peregrine Walsingham. Aged seventy. Suddenly, at The Priory, Little Diddingcote, Berkshire. Leaves a widow and one son." Ah yes. That's the fellow.

Mary draws a bold circle on the page

Felicity is looking at a boldly-circled notice in the Obituary column of Mary's Telegraph. *She is puzzled*

Felicity (*reading aloud*) "Robert Peregrine Walsingham. Aged seventy. Suddenly at The Priory, Little Diddingcote, Berkshire. Leaves a widow and one son." (*Thoughtfully*) Why has she circled *that* name? Robert Peregrine Walsingham ... Why has she — marked him down?

Mary begins to draft a letter

Mary (*speaking as she writes*) Dear Robert, I am so worried. Why haven't you been in touch this quarter. (*She makes a correction*) No. (*Continuing*) I can't think what has happened. The usual hasn't arrived and it is such a bad moment. I'd never write but it is urgent. Poor little Bobbie has been having a lot more of his ... (*She thinks*) Attacks? Yes, attacks. (*She goes on writing*) He is such a long-suffering ... (*Correcting it*) Brave little chap. I know I promised never to write but I feel sure the bank or post office have made some bad mistake ... (*She stops writing and yawns*) No rush.

Felicity stares at the newspaper: realization gradually dawning. She seizes the phone and excitedly stabs a number. Mary puts the draft letter, marker pen, pencil and newspaper in the holdall. Then she takes out a sunhat and sunglasses and puts them on the table

Felicity (*into the phone*) Louise? Oh, Louise, the most wonderful thing has happened! It was all wrong! About Edward. It was all lies. There was no *affaire*. There was no child. Sick or otherwise. There was not a word of truth in it! ...

Mary exits DR

(*Into the phone*) Never mind how I found out. But I'm absolutely certain. Never mind how I know. Louise. ... Louise. ... Oh, very well. Listen. The woman came here. Yes! Arrived on my doorstep! To apologize. Yes! … Yes, you're right. I finished up sorry for her. But that's not the point. She accidently left her newspaper behind. And she'd marked a name in the Obituary column. … What? … No, Louise. But it looks like a wealthy family. It must be another victim! Don't you see? The whole thing was a confidence trick. … Louise, I was never more sure of anything in my life. ... Why? Well, I just am, that's all. … Yes. … Well. … All right, you've guessed. Yes, I did part with money. … Never mind how much. … No, I'm not going to try and get it back! No. No, Louise. … No. …

Mary enters DR. *She is wearing a sundress. She is carrying an exotic-looking drink, topped with a tiny sunshade. She puts on her sunhat and sunglasses and settles down in the chair, sipping the drink*

(*Into the phone*) I don't begrudge a penny of it, Louise. Knowing that Edward was everything we ever believed, that's what's important. The money is nothing. I know I won't hear anything about the matter again. And nor must anyone else! Ever! You gave your word of honour, remember? Oh, Louise, how could I have doubted him? I knew him through and through! But then that woman was a professional. Through and through. You do see? … Where is she now? A good question. I imagine she's lounging on some exotic island. Hawaii possibly. Sipping a drink from a coconut and getting a rich tan. Who cares! … No, Louise, I don't feel a fool. I feel light-headed. Light-headed! I'm so, so thankful! … Bye! (*She puts aside the phone. She clasps the locket to her chest; through laughter and tears*) Edward … Oh, my dear …

Mary is chuckling, with self-satisfaction. She downs her drink

Mary (*beckoning off stage* R) Steward! I'll have another of these, if you please. And you can make it a double, OK?

The CURTAIN *falls*

CRUISE MISSILE

CHARACTERS

Goldie
Janet

Scene — the deck of a cruise liner
Time — the present

The deck of a cruise liner. A sunny day

When the CURTAIN *rises two empty deckchairs are set beside each other,* C

Janet enters R. *She is in her early sixties, perhaps. She is uncertain of herself. She wears a beach coat, a very practical sun hat and has on dark glasses. She carries a large blue towel, a pretty canvas bag and holds a little card in her hand which she is using to check her whereabouts on the ship. She moves tentatively to* C, *peering around, stumbling against one of the chairs*

Janet Oh, I beg your pardon. (*She sees it is empty*) Oh. Ah. (*She crosses to* L *and speaks to someone off. She indicates the empty chairs*) Is anyone sitting here? ... What? ... Er ... I said is anyone sitting in these chairs? I mean ... I know they're empty right now. But I thought someone might be coming back or ... I wouldn't like to take anyone's seat ... Well, I'll chance it. (*She lays the blue towel out on the chair and takes off her beach coat, revealing a modest sundress. She puts the bag down beside the chair and begins to study her little card; muttering, pointing out front*) Now there's the sea there. The ship is going that way. I think. (*She steps forward to check*) Yes. So that is the front end and that is the back end. I'm on the Games Deck. I think. (*She squints about*) Yes. Here I am. Lovely. (*She returns to her seat, takes a book from her bag and settles down contentedly*)

A voice calls "Yoo hoo" from off R

Janet is startled. The book flies from her hands. She gives a little moan. Pulling her hat down over her face, she turns on her side feigning sleep

Goldie appears, R. *She is much the same age as Janet. She is a flamboyant lady. Her cruisewear is a knock-out and she totters in on high-rise sandals, carrying a huge golden holdall and blue towel*

Goldie Yoo, hoo! I thought it was you! I've been trailing you all over the place.
Janet I was trying to familiarize myself with the ship. With the help of the little guide.
Goldie Oh you needn't bother with that, you can always ask me. I know this ship like the back of my hand. Now where were you making for?
Janet Nowhere special. Somewhere quiet to sit down.

Goldie Well, this is quiet enough. Why don't we sit here? I'll tell you all about the layout of the decks and all that.
Janet I wouldn't want to put you to the trouble.
Goldie Not at all. I like to make newcomers feel at home.

Goldie dumps down her things and spreads her blue towel on the chair by Janet

Janet I think that chair is taken.
Goldie Nonsense, there's no-one in it. Finders keepers. You've a lot to learn about cruising. Think of me as your guide and mentor. Now isn't this nice?
Janet Yes.
Goldie Aren't you glad you met me?
Janet Yes.
Goldie Now, you see these big blue towels?
Janet Yes.
Goldie They're for putting on the chairs for relaxing. But the brown ones are for swimming and sunbathing. They can take a lot more sun oil, you know. Have you got enough of them in your cabin?
Janet I think so.
Goldie Let me know if you haven't. I've got plenty in my cabin. And at home. (*She chortles*)
Janet (*puzzled*) Are we allowed to take them then?

Goldie gives her an unbelieving look

I have a very good book. I got it from the ship's library after breakfast.
Goldie I wondered where you disappeared to. I came back with some more croissants and you'd gone.
Janet I'm sorry. I'd had enough. I mean, I wanted to get on with the day. There seems to be so much to do.
Goldie I'll help you there. Did you get your programme under your door last night?
Janet Oh, I did, yes. But I thought I'd better take it easy at first.
Goldie Nonsense, you want to get your money's worth, don't you? I've got my programme with me here and we'll plan things together. (*She rummages in her bag for her programme*)
Janet (*weakly*) You really needn't, you know.
Goldie Happy to, dear. I'm an old hand. I know all the wrinkles.
Janet But we may not like the same things.
Goldie That's what I mean, you have to try everything. Now, do you know where we are?
Janet Er …
Goldie We're steaming at twenty-one-point-six knots. Did you put your watch forward?

Janet Yes, I ——

Goldie Which tours are you taking? It's two hundred and forty nautical miles from Agadir to Lanzarote.

Janet I hadn't decided yet.

Goldie Oh, you have to get booked. Don't worry. I'll do it for you. I know the Purser rather well. Shall we go ashore at Tenerife? It's very interesting. I bought the sweetest tablemats. Cost practically nothing.

Janet Isn't there a volcano?

Goldie (*laughing*) A volcano? I hope not.

Janet But ——

Goldie Now you are not to worry. They'd never put you in any danger, I must say that for them. Are you into keep fit?

Janet It depends …

Goldie I like to take a jog round the games deck. How about that?

Janet I thought I might just promenade around the promenade deck …

Goldie Or there's the gym. The gym has everything — including a dishy instructor. Very good for you.

Janet Not right now perhaps, but please don't let me stop you …

Goldie No no. We'll get plenty of exercise, I guarantee.

Janet I believe there's a get-together for those travelling alone …

Goldie Oh, you've missed that. Anyway, you don't want to bother with all those singles. They're terribly boring

Janet They can't *all* be boring. Not every trip. And anyway I'm one and you're one.

Goldie Yes. And we're very lucky to have chummed up so soon. We won't need any of the others, see?

Janet There was a rather nice gentleman on my table last night who said he would be there and ——

Goldie Trust me, Janet. Will you trust me? I've met all these single men.

Janet He said he might be at the talk about the port where we go ashore on Wednesday …

Goldie I've been to all the port talks, Janet. I can tell you all you need to know, I promise you.

Janet Yes, Goldie.

Goldie consults the programme

Goldie Oh good, there's a lovely singalong later. I love a singalong. People always comment on my strong voice.

Janet (*quickly*) I haven't any voice at all.

Goldie What a shame. There's a chiropody demonstration.

Janet (*recoiling*) Chiropody?

Goldie It's on at the same time.

Janet Ah, then I'll go to that.
Goldie Not the singalong with me?
Janet No, I'd simply love to go to the chiropody demonstration.
Goldie It's in the beauty room. I'll show you how to get there.
Janet I'll find it. I'll find it. Truly!
Goldie You said that about your Lifeboat Drill, didn't you, Janet? Yet there you were running about like a headless chicken looking for your muster station.
Janet I hadn't quite worked out the layout of the ship.
Goldie Just as well I spotted you, wasn't it? And took you along with me.
Janet Yes, but ——
Goldie And showed you how to put on your lifejacket.
Janet But I think we were meant to be shown by a crew member.
Goldie So, I saved us all a lot of time, didn't I? Didn't I, Janet? Admit it.
Janet I suppose so. I still think I was at the wrong muster station. I was at yours, not mine.
Goldie Your muster station is clearly written on the back of your cabin door, Janet.
Janet That's what I mean.
Goldie Oh, really, Janet. We're not on the *Titanic*.
Janet I hope not.
Goldie You are a scream. You just stay close by me, I've been on more cruises … ! Ha ha! I know the ropes, Janet, trust me. Now what's the plan?
Janet I thought I'd just sit here for a bit.
Goldie Now that's definitely not the attitude. You can sit about any old time. Now what about line-dancing? You'll enjoy that.
Janet It does sound quite jolly. But I've never done any …
Goldie You'll pick it up in no time. Look, I'll give you an idea. Get up …
Janet Tell you what, you give me a demonstration. I'm sure you're very good.
Goldie Leave it to Goldie! (*She stands up and moves to front. She takes up a stance*) You watch me. Thumbs in waistband and get into cowboy mode. Right? (*She demonstrates*)

Seeing Goldie is now carried away Janet returns sneakily to her book. Goldie prances on, takes a final stylish whirl and comes to a stop

There!
Janet That really was most helpful, Goldie.
Goldie I'm quite a good coach. I'll help you at the salsa class too, if you like. (*She sits and picks up the programme*) Now, what is our schedule for later? Tonight's the welcome reception. I've already booked a session in the beauty salon. And I told them you'd probably be there too. Best to be in first.

Janet I don't think ——

Goldie They're marvellous girls. I know them all. You must go. They can do miracles.

Janet Maybe later in the week …

Goldie What are you wearing tonight, Janet? It's formal, you know.

Janet Yes, I know.

Goldie I have this two-piece in royal blue sequins. And I'll have them do my hair up with an extra piece. When we get into hotter climes I have my pink silk chiffon with feathers (*demonstrating*) here and here. It just floats as I dance. Floats. What have you brought for the black and white ball, Janet?

Janet I ——

Goldie I can probably lend you something. I always bring far too many clothes. And then I go and buy a whole lot more from the shop. Aren't I naughty?! Did you see the shop yet? Lovely things.

Janet I haven't had time to see them properly.

Goldie Well when you do I'll come along. Nothing like having someone else's opinion, is there?

Janet Nothing like it.

Goldie Cruisewear is quite special you see. Not like normal wear at all.

Janet It does seem more colourful.

Goldie Just watch the men's shirts on the tropical night. You can get your sight injured! But it's so cheerful. The brilliant sunlight makes colours look less bright, you see. For instance, that sundress of yours, I'm sure you thought it very pretty when you bought it.

Janet Yes, I did.

Goldie And I bet you never thought how drab it would look on the deck of a cruiseliner.

Janet No, I can't say I did.

Goldie Don't tell me, I bet you've brought a plain black swimsuit. Right?

Janet Right.

Goldie Oh, I'll have lots of fun finding you something more exciting.

Janet But ——

Goldie Believe me, I was just as dowdy when I came on my first cruise. You quickly learn.(*Indicating her outfit*) How about this then? Stunning or what!

Janet Stunning.

Goldie I wish my husband could see me now.

Janet What a pity he couldn't come with you.

Goldie That wouldn't have been possible, Janet. He's dead.

Janet I'm so sorry. I hadn't realized you were a widow.

Goldie Quite a while now. That's why I took up cruising. We never had the money before. But he had this very big insurance policy, you see, so I've been enjoying it.

Janet I'm sure he would have been glad.

Goldie Oh, it's what he would have wanted, Janet. He worked so hard all his life. He was a lovely man, Janet. Very good to me. Whenever he was at home.

Janet I believe it's getting warmer.

Goldie Well, it would. We're going due south.

Janet I thought I might go ashore at Vigo …

Goldie Waste of time, my dear. All those natives and nothing but smelly stalls filled with junk.

Janet But I'd like to see some of the local colour.

Goldie Wait until we get to Madeira. Madeira's lovely.

Janet I have been to Madeira.

Goldie Oh, really? I thought you were a first-time traveller.

Janet No, I'm a first-time cruiser.

Goldie Ah. Well, you've chosen the right ship. Now, what sort of things do you enjoy?

Janet I tell you what, er, Goldie. You tell me what *you* enjoy.

Goldie Oh, that's sweet, Janet. You're going to choose the same things so that we can go together. Well, I like practically everything.

Janet Oh. I believe there's a classical recital on Wednesday.

Goldie Oh yes, he plays the piano wonderfully. And it gives you a chance for a little snooze before the Gala Variety Show and the late night Chocoholics Buffet. But let's think about this morning. Eh, Janet?

Janet Yes, Goldie.

Goldie There are adult deck sports at ten thirty.

Janet (*startled*) Adult deck sports? Sounds rather — early in the trip.

Goldie It's quoits, Janet. Quoits. I'm beginning to think you're a dark horse.

Janet No, no. (*Laughing nervously*) What you see is what you get. I'm really a very ordinary person.

Goldie Well, never mind.

Janet And I don't think I've got the right shoes for line dancing. (*Quickly*) And I have very difficult feet.

Goldie All right then, I'll go to the line dancing this morning. And you can go to the alternative. And I'll collect you later so we can play the slot machines and put some money on the Tote. (*Reading the programme*) Now, you're going to make "an attractive key-ring in cross-stitch. Bring your own scissors."

Janet I'm going to what?

Goldie The alternative activity to line dancing — handicrafts. It's very popular, Janet. I made a pulled-thread bookmark on my first cruise. I've got it still.

Janet Is there a rule that says I can't just do nothing? I saw some people quietly relaxing in the sun.

Goldie But it's an opportunity to make new friends. Don't you want to make new friends, Janet?

Janet Yes, I do. Well, I did.

Goldie I'll introduce you to the woman who does the handicrafts —

Janet Goldie, I'm having second thoughts about line dancing.

Goldie Oh good. Buy some soft shoes of some sort. There's a lot of stamping, you see, and we might all go through the deck. One of the officers explained it to me …

Janet I hope he was joking.

Goldie (*thoughtfully*) Come to think of it, maybe he was. I remember, he told me the afternoon film was *The Poseidon Adventure*. Yes, I think he was! The naughty boy. They're very sweet, the ship's officers. They really put themselves out for us. Mind you, it's probably part of their contract. Giving the lone ladies a whirl.

Janet I wouldn't like to think that.

Goldie Why not? Make use of them, dear. After all it's no hardship with girls like us! I suppose it's a bit of a drag with some of the terrible old freaks.

Janet I have a very handsome cabin steward.

Goldie Mine's an old friend. He'll do anything for me. Whatever time of the day or night, if I need a little snack or whatever, I only have to call. The ship's doctor's a darling too.

Janet I hope I won't need him.

Goldie You never know. He's the one with the red bits. I'll point him out. Last voyage, in the Bay of Biscay, half the passengers were writhing in their cabins. But there he was dancing the night away in the Dolphin Disco. Such stamina.

Janet The sea seems very calm so far.

Goldie But it's amazing how quickly a squall can come up.

Janet (*apprehensively*) Really?

Goldie (*rising*) Come here and I'll show you something.

Goldie pulls Janet to her feet and they move DS

Look out towards the horizon.

Janet does so

What can you see? Mm?

Janet (*peering*) A seagull?

Goldie No, Janet.

Janet No? A guillemot? Not an albatross!

Goldie No, no. You can see waves. Waves.

Janet Well, of course.

Goldie Now, you count them …

Janet There are an awful lot of them … I don't think …

Goldie Concentrate, Janet. Every seventh wave is a bit bigger than the others, see?

Janet I take your word for it, Goldie.

Goldie Now, when the sea is rough it's the seventh wave you have to watch out for. And when it's really mountainous and the waves are rearing up way over the ship, then it will be the seventh wave that finally swamps over the side. Old sea-dogs know all about the seventh wave. They fear the seventh wave. When they're tossing about in a gigantic storm they dread the seventh wave.

Janet If it's such a gigantic storm I'm surprised they have time to count.

Goldie Never underestimate the ocean, Janet.

Janet I wouldn't dream of it. I'm just not too keen to think about it right now, when it looks all blue and glittering, with little white flecks of foam. And the boat is so steady …

Goldie Ship, Janet. Ship. Don't let the captain hear you call it a boat.

Janet I don't expect to meet the captain.

Goldie Indeed you will. I'll introduce you.

Janet (*uncertainly*) That will be nice.

Goldie We got very friendly two — no, three trips ago. We danced together. I was Carmen Miranda. I had all these bananas on my head. I got them from a galley steward. Such a dear.

Janet It was fancy dress?

Goldie Yes Janet, of course! I don't go around all the time with bananas on my head.

Janet Sorry Goldie, I was getting confused. Thinking about storms and what if the ship turned upside down like in that film. I'm sure I couldn't find my way out right side up, let alone upside down.

Goldie A ship *capsizes*, Janet. It doesn't turn upside down, it *capsizes*.

Janet I'd really like to sit down, Goldie.

Goldie I don't think you're a very good sailor, Janet, are you?

Janet (*bridling a little*) Well, if the crew all get washed overboard by your seventh wave, let's say I'm not offering to drive the ship.

Goldie You don't drive a ship.

Janet Well, whatever you do to make it go! And whatever it is, I'm sure *you'll* be capable of taking the helm and bringing us into port! (*She sits*)

Goldie (*sitting beside her*) Whatever is the matter with you, Janet?

Janet I'm sorry, that was very impolite.

Goldie Quite uncalled for.

Janet Yes. Please forgive me.

Goldie No excuse for bad manners.

Janet No. It was all the talk of being shipwrecked …

Goldie We won't be shipwrecked.
Janet And being seasick …
Goldie You won't be seasick.
Janet I hope not.
Goldie You mustn't even think about it.
Janet No, silly of me.
Goldie The worst thing you can do is dwell on the idea.
Janet You're absolutely right. (*Firmly*) I am not going to be seasick.
Goldie Of course you aren't.
Janet No.
Goldie And if you are, I have some wonderful pills to fix you up the minute you feel queazy. (*She spots someone in the distance and waves*) Oh, look, there's Mrs Bellchamber. (*Calling*) Hallo, there! Hallo!
Janet Do go and talk to your friend … I'll just …

Janet makes to leave. Goldie pins her down with one hand while still waving with the other

Goldie (*smiling and calling*) Sailing away again, Mrs Bellchamber! (*Muttering to Janet*) Take a look at her, Janet. Take a look!
Janet I won't be in the least offended …
Goldie Stay put, Janet! This is rich! (*Calling out again*) Have a good day! (*She settles back with a triumphant little giggle*) Well! Did you see that woman, Janet? And the man she was with?
Janet Yes.
Goldie Do you know who that was?
Janet Mr Bellchamber?
Goldie Not on your life. But they're sharing a cabin again, I'll bet. I met her last trip. And we got talking, as one does. She was holidaying alone because Mr Bellchamber hates the sea, she said. And she was late booking so she had to take a double cabin, she said. And guess what, her cabin mate turned out to be a man. Mr Antrobus. Well, they made the best of it and got along very well, she said. And all us old hands thought "fun — ny", but we gave her the benefit of the doubt.
Janet I suppose it could happen.
Goldie Oh, yes. Once. But, get this, she's sharing her cabin again on this trip with, surprise, surprise, Mr Antrobus.
Janet You mean she's left Mr Bellchamber?
Goldie Hardly. Mr Bellchamber is a merchant banker. It's all happened by chance again, she says. Well, ho ho, is all I say. It'll be the talk of the ship, you see.
Janet Maybe if we don't mention it.
Goldie Janet! You're no fun at all!

Janet Well …

Goldie What you have to realize is that a cruise ship is a world of its own. Throw your inhibitions overboard … And forgive me, Janet, but I'd say you have plenty!

Janet Then maybe you'd better find somebody more congenial …

Janet makes to move. Goldie restrains her

Goldie No, no. I consider it a challenge. I'll get you going, you see. Would you like something to drink? Or eat? I can get a steward, they're always flitting around.

Janet No, thanks. I had a huge breakfast. I must say, the food seems to be excellent.

Goldie You've seen nothing, yet! Local specialities as we go on. Every sort of choice on offer for lunch and for dinner. And gorgeous creamy cakes for tea and a midnight barbecue most nights. It's feeding on demand on this ship! (*She looks off stage* R) You know I believe they've got their mid-morning coffee over there. Are you sure you won't …?

Janet No truly.

Goldie Will you mind if I …?

Janet Please, please, do go along.

Goldie rises and exits R

Janet gives a sigh and opens her book

Goldie appears again

Goldie I'll be back quite soon, Janet. Don't feel I've abandoned you!

Janet (*looking up from her book*) No, of course not. What a thought.

Goldie exits

Janet takes up her book for a moment, then looks furtively off R. *She establishes that Goldie is out of sight, then begins gathering up her possessions, quickly stuffing them into her bag. She rises and puts on her beachcoat and is just about to make her escape* L

Goldie enters L. *She is carrying a tray of coffee*

Janet stops in her tracks

Goldie Janet! Where are you off to?

Janet I — wanted to write cards — forgot my pen — going to my cabin …
Goldie I have a pen, Janet. You don't have to go trailing off to your cabin. Sit down, do. I brought you a coffee anyway. A steward was passing and I grabbed his tray.
Janet But, weren't they for someone else?
Goldie Oh, he can easily get some more.

Janet returns to her seat and sits down. Goldie gives her a cup of coffee and then seats herself

Choccy bikkies too. Yum yum.
Janet (*resigned*) Yum yum.

They both sip their coffee. Goldie munches her biscuit

Goldie Now eat up that biscuit, Janet. You look as if you could do with feeding up a bit. I was kidding about putting on weight. Anyway you'll burn it off. We'll go to early morning workout together. Before breakfast. If I remember rightly, and I do, tomorrow morning it's legs, tums and bums!
Janet Legs, tums and … I'm really not sure I'm up to it.
Goldie That's very defeatist. You need taking in hand. You know, I spotted you the moment you came aboard. I said, there's a woman who doesn't look too fit. There's a woman hasn't had an easy life. There's a woman who's saved hard for this holiday and she needs to get all she can out of it. I said to myself, that's a very vulnerable person. I said, there's a woman who'll get stuck with a stuffed turtle.
Janet A *turtle*?
Goldie A turtle.
Janet A *stuffed* turtle?
Goldie A stuffed turtle. It's illegal to bring stuffed turtles into the UK, you see. So don't *think* of getting one.
Janet I wasn't! I assure you.
Goldie Well, people do. And then they get stopped at Customs and have to surrender them. Or they throw them overboard.
Janet I'm glad you told me. I'd hate to look out of a porthole and get hit by a stuffed turtle.
Goldie I don't suppose you will. I love the sea. Did I tell you I went on the final voyage of the *Candida*? And as we left each port for the last time, all the little tugs came out sounding their hooters. And made arcs of water with their hoses. As if they were crying tears. And *Candida* sounded her foghorn so mournfully. Like a great beast dying.
Janet How sad.

Goldie Yes. (*Pause, then briskly*) But it was high time they scrapped her. Poor old tub, only held together by her paintwork. Definitely due for the knackers yard.
Janet Who?
Goldie The *Candida*, Janet.
Janet Oh. I thought you'd seen another friend.
Goldie No no. So here we are on this splendid new ship. Isn't she great?
Janet Yes. I think it's a really beautiful vessel.
Goldie She. She, Janet. Ships are feminine. I knew you were a first-timer by your lost look I said, it's my duty to give her a bit of useful advice. For instance, warn her not to make close friends with anyone too early or she'll get stuck with them.
Janet I see.
Goldie And most important, to get the right cabin. By the way where is your cabin? Are you sharing with nice people?
Janet No …
Goldie Ah, now you don't have to put up with that. I know the Purser, and we can have a word …
Janet No, no. I didn't mean that. I'm not sharing with anyone …
Goldie Oh? Don't tell me you haven't got a cabin mate …
Janet (*quickly*) No, I have an outside single cabin on A Deck and I am wonderfully comfortable.
Goldie Well! I should think you are! Well!! (*Curiously*) Did you say you were a widow?
Janet No, I didn't.
Goldie Ah, divorced! Did he run off with another woman!
Janet No …
Goldie He didn't run off with another man!
Janet No …
Goldie Come on, you can tell me. It'll go no further.
Janet I told you, I'm not at all an interesting person.
Goldie I know! You've won the Lottery!
Janet I've *not* won the Lottery!
Goldie (*crossly*) Really, Janet, I've run out of ideas. I've never known anyone so secretive! It's a good job for you I'm not *some* people! Some people would probe and probe!
Janet I'm an ordinary married woman, Goldie.
Goldie Separated?
Janet *No!* My husband had to go to Brussels for two weeks on business. And he and the children suggested I took this holiday to set me up. Because I'd had a little op.
Goldie You know, you're right. That's not very interesting.
Janet I *told* you.

Goldie (*hopefully*) What was the op.?
Janet I had a polyp removed.
Goldie A polyp? Was it up your … ?
Janet Up my nose.
Goldie I might have guessed.
Janet Boring, I agree, it was quite unnecessary to make a fuss about. But the family knew I had always wanted a voyage on a big ship. So they secretly arranged it. Before we all get involved in the arrangements for our son's wedding in September. Do you have children?
Goldie Never felt the need.
Janet I expect mine will all be making shore-to-ship calls to me. And my husband sent a big bunch of flowers to my cabin.
Goldie Nice.
Janet My son is an accountant in the City. And my daughter is in computers. They've done so well.
Goldie Still I expect you're glad to be shot of them all for a couple of weeks.
Janet Not at all. We're very close. My daughter is keeping my plants watered.
Goldie I don't have to bother with a garden now. I live in an apartment and we pay the management for all that, thank goodness.
Janet But the first new potatoes are delicious. Straight from the earth, scrubbed, then into the saucepan with a sprig of mint. We have raspberry canes and gooseberries and plums and apples, of course. And I have a damson bush. I love damson preserve. Do you make preserves?
Goldie No, I don't.
Janet I love trying out new recipes on the family. But my son always demands steak and kidney pudding. I know some people put in ox kidney but I use lamb kidney and mushrooms. We have an Aga of course. Do you use gas or electric, Goldie?
Goldie I like to leave domestic matters at home for the duration of the voyage.
Janet My prospective daughter-in-law made all the finger eats for their engagement party.
Goldie Fancy.
Janet Now we're all set for the wedding. My son announced it quite suddenly.
Goldie (*interest rekindled*) He's got her pregnant?
Janet No, nothing like that. He heard of an excellent holiday offer in Cuba. Just the thing for their honeymoon. Her parents are really charming. They have a villa in the Algarve. I expect we'll all take holidays together. The men will have their golf. Would you like to see a photograph of my husband? I have one here. (*She fumbles in her bag*) Oh, no it must be in the cabin.

Goldie Never mind.

Janet I have one of my daughter and son too. And our dog. He died earlier this year.

Goldie Run over?

Janet No …

Goldie Poisoned?

Janet Of course not! Old age. Just went quietly to sleep. But he'd been one of the family.

Goldie I can see that.

Janet I have a picture of my son and daughter playing in the garden with the dog and the neighbour's children. I'll go and get it to show you.

Goldie Don't bother yourself now, Janet.

Janet It's no bother. There's one of them swinging on an apple tree. Did I tell you we have apple trees?

Goldie Yes. Yes, you did.

Janet My husband made a treehouse for the children. You can just see the remains of it in one of the photos of my old aunt. She's wearing a big sunhat. She had a delicate skin. I'll just go and get those photographs. There's one of my brother-in-law. That's my sister's husband and ——

Goldie (*rising*) No! Now Janet, you are not to budge. I've just remembered, I must have a word with ——

Janet (*restraining Goldie*) Don't go, I've hardly started — I must just tell you about my curtains for the wedding.

Goldie You're wearing curtains?

Janet My husband and I decided we must have the house done over because we'll be having several relations staying. And a cousin of the bride's mother … We've done one room in peachy white with … with …

Goldie Janet, I do believe it's time for my injection. (*She consults her watch*) Yes, it certainly is. (*She rises and gathers her belongings*)

Janet Injection? Nothing serious, I hope?

Goldie I'm not sure. But if you don't see me around for the rest of the voyage, you'll know it was more serious than I expected.

Janet (*rising*) Poor you! Wouldn't you like me to come and keep you company?

Goldie No, no! I have to go to sick bay. I may be some time.

Janet (*detaining Goldie by the sleeve*) All the more reason ——

Goldie (*very earnestly*) It may be contagious, Janet. I've been waiting to hear.

Janet Oh, dear. I'd never have guessed.

Goldie I've tried to be brave.

Janet Isn't there anything I can do?

Goldie (*bravely*) Just enjoy yourself, Janet.

Janet Well. It's been nice meeting you. I suppose we'd better not shake hands.

Goldie Pardon? Oh, yes. We'd better not.
Janet In case you're ever in my area. I'll give you my address. (*She fumbles in her bag*) Oh dear, it's in my cabin.
Goldie I'm never in that area.
Janet What a shame. Ships that pass, eh?
Goldie Ships that pass. Goodbye.

Goldie exits R

Janet (*calling after Goldie*) Goodbye, Goldie. I'll keep an eye out for you! Best of luck! (*She waves until Goldie has gone. She returns to her seat, picks up her book and finds her page. She takes a last peer off* R, *then she looks towards the* L; *beckoning and calling*) Steward! May I have a large G and T! (*She turns to the front, gives a smile of victory and settles down to read her book*)

The CURTAIN *falls*

FURNITURE AND PROPERTY LIST

Cupboard Love

On stage: Two beachchairs

Personal: **Peggy**: light bumbag containing a comb, mirror and lipstick; a small towel
Jane: light bumbag containing small water bottle

Last Post

On stage: Garden table. *On it*: a tray with a small coffee percolator filled with coffee, a pretty cup and saucer, milk jug and sugar
Two beachchairs
Small table
Chair

Off stage: Several unopened letters, one envelope blue; *The Times* newspaper; cordless telephone (**Felicity**)
Pen, blue notepad and envelope (**Mary**)
Cream-coloured unopened letter (**Mary**)
Pen, cream notepaper and envelope (**Felicity**)
Handbag and copy of the *Telegraph* (**Mary**)
Handbag containing a chequebook and pen (**Felicity**)
Holdall containing the *Telegraph,* a marker pen, a notepad and pen, sunhat, sunglasses (**Mary**)
Exotic-looking drink, topped with tiny sunshade (**Mary**)

Personal: **Felicity**: locket, handkerchief

Cruise Missile

On stage: Two deckchairs

Off stage: Large blue towel, pretty canvas bag containing book, a small plan of the ship (**Janet**)
Huge golden holdall containing programme, blue towel (**Goldie**)
Tray of coffee and biscuits (**Goldie**)

LIGHTING PLOT

Cupboard Love

To open: Exterior lighting, early sunny morning effect

No cues

Last Post

Cue 1	**Mary** enters *Bring up spotlight on* **Mary**, *lighting table and chair* DR	(Page 20)
Cue 2	**Mary** seals the envelope and exits *Fade spotlight* DR	(Page 21)
Cue 3	**Felicity** exits *Bring up spotlight* DR	(Page 22)
Cue 4	**Felicity** begins to read the *Telegraph* *Bring up spotlight on table and chair* DR	(Page 28)

Cruise Missile

To open: Exterior lighting, sunny effect

No cues

EFFECTS PLOT

Cupboard Love

No cues

Last Post

Cue 1	**Felicity** begins to read a letter *The telephone rings*	(Page 19)
Cue 2	**Felicity** picks up the letter and reads *The telephone rings*	(Page 20)
Cue 3	**Felicity** stands staring at **Mary** *The door slams*	(Page 23)

Cruise Missile

No cues